NOVEMBER BECAME SPRING

november became spring

KYLE ERIN

Seasons Publishing

This is me. heart, mind, & soul. It's joy and sadness. Random thoughts, embarrassing moments, and poorly constructed advice.

Read at own risk.

Enjoy.

Dedication

For my friends who support me and my family who built me.

To Tyler, my friend and my editor, my wordsmith and fellowship.

To those who choose to read this- you are loved and you are cherished. I hope these words make you feel that.

Preface

I want to start by saying thank you. To you- the person who has undoubtedly been counting down the days until this book was published. And while that last sentence is probably not true, you chose to pick up this book.

I hope you're encouraged. Humbled, comforted, contemplative; maybe a little convicted. Most of all, I want you to know that what you feel is felt by others too. You don't have fight battles alone.

The following comes from a journal entry I wrote on May 1, 2020.

Morning-

another bad night.

But I got up. At 7am. I went for a run. I hated it. I showered and ate a banana. And a lot of peanut butter. Not great, but better. I'm okay, I know I'll be ok. I need a routine. I need to make my own stability. I'm stuck at home (hello pandemic).

It wasn't easy. More often than not, I had to force myself to write. It consisted of procrastination, lots of coffee, f--- words, regression, tears, laughs, and an unbelievable amount of accountability. The vulnerability was hard. I stayed up late, woke up early. I kept messing with my words and overthinking it all. But I'm not the same person who wrote that journal entry on May 1, 2020. I'm stronger, bolder, and can provide you with at least eight different banana bread recipes.

Change itself is inevitable and trying to fight it or being afraid of it is something that holds us back. It can be about the big and the small; the choices you never meant to make.

This collection isn't really about those kinds of moments, but more about what comes from them. Where the pain goes, why the sadness lingers, but also how the joy is able to come alive again. It's about being okay when things don't end up the way you wanted them to, but knowing it's the way they needed to.

Slowly and purposefully, I grew. spring turned into summer. I let summer become fall. And then, all at once, november became spring.

Imagination breeds stories.
Vulnerability brings maturity.
Writing our stories gives others a chance to learn.
Stories help to step out of reality for a time,
and become a part of an adventure.

Isn't that what we all want?
To be a part of something that's bigger than us?
To feel like the world is a never-ending exploration?

Take your moments and cherish them.
Remember the good and learn from the bad.

- *authors*

Spring.

I want to be your person.
I want to be genuine.
I want to be real.
Trust me with your weaknesses and I will do the same.
This is what I thought I wanted.

All pain has purpose.
That's what they've always said.
But I can't figure out why,
you thought it was your job to teach me that.
To turn what I thought would last forever
into something that's forever dead.

- this is what I thought I wanted

All the self-doubt and the anxiety.
The moments when I feel so alone,
paralyzed in my skin.
The moments when I'm not fun and spontaneous
like the girl you know,
but instead wants to fall into the hole
I've been digging all my life.
I'm asking you to love me in those moments.
Moments when I'm easily aggravated, quiet,
indifferent.

When I push you away,
I need you to hold on even tighter.

And I will love you for it, even deeper.

   *- **that's how we began***

I want to love you.
Just because it's what I'm meant to do.
And when you walked out,
so did my purpose.

- at least that's how I felt

I was hoping this was it.
I was so tired of starting over.
He said he loved me; I believed it.
My heart was tempted.
It was fooled. It was gaslit.

He didn't love me, but craved the way I made him feel.
He loved that he could push my boundaries
and I didn't fight back.
He loved that he could say, "I love you,"
and that disappeared the disrespect.
The "I love you's" buried all the doubt,
as he relished in my body.
He loved that he had power.

And then he'd leave me more broken than before.
But still wanting more.

   - losing my ground

Sometimes, you were an angel.
Sometimes, you weren't.
I never knew which one I was going to get.
And I kind of liked that...

- temptation

Call me to tell me about your day.
Call me when you're sad.
Call me when you're overwhelmed.
Call me every time you want to.
I am your girl.
The one Van Morrison sung about.
The one whose heart will continue to grow for you.

- my deepest desires

Oh, how I wish it was easy.
How I wish it was good.
You'd show me the person you could be,
the one I loved with all my heart.

But the man I had in private
is not who I had in public.
I grasped for the potential of you,
but settled for your reality.

- i settled when I should have run

Memories and feelings.
They're simple.

It's as simple as saying:

I want to hold your hand,
walk by your side,
sing your favorite song,
watch you smile,
watch you grow,
watch you try to cook,
and listen to you talk about your day.
I want to be your family and your home.

It's that simple.
I want you to kiss me in the rain,
touch me like I'm brand new,
hold me like you never want to let me go.
Open your heart to me and I'll give mine to you.

It's that simple.

- then why is this so complicated?

You ruined red for me.

When sleepovers with red vines
became hangovers with cheap wine.
And you ruined red for me.

Red flags were invisible
when it came to you.
Red lipstick was my favorite,
before I learned it was your favorite too.

Red skies at night, red m&ms on the counter.
Valentines stained the floor
with red petals,
a secret behind our bedroom door.

Red made me smile,
it held power; it held love.
But you crumpled that up.
My tower was falling,
you emptied my cup.
I was now muted,
but screaming in my head,
mourning for how I'd forever view red.

You ruined red for me.

- the color red

Was I not enough?
What was I missing?
Why wasn't I good for you?
Why can't I forget the way you made me feel?
It keeps circling me,
squeezing tighter as it sees me breathing easier.
It's an evil that knows when to strike.
A weed that refuses to shrivel.
It's what you left me with,
but it's what I'm learning to break free from.

- pleasing, pleasing, pleasing

When your heart aches, will you feel it?
Will you let it in?
Everything you ran from,
will you let your guard down?
Just this once, just for me.

You were good to me.
You wanted nothing but success for me.
You wanted only me.
Until you didn't.

- you changed your mind

I was once asked the question:
"Do you face arguments with compassion or anger?"
Neither.
I avoid them.
If I disagree, people will leave.
That lie I've believed all my life.
And still do.
So, I stay silent.
Even when I should scream.
Why?

Because I don't want to be alone.

- *confrontation*

Is it naïve to just want someone who wants you?
Who will care to break down your walls?
Who thinks you're worth that?

I want to be taken care of,
but will never ask for that.

I want to be noticed, but won't step into a spotlight.
I like surprises, but pretend I don't.
What I show isn't always what's true.

I have so much to give,
but give to the wrong people.

    - the fear of something that's real

I wasn't myself for months.
And people noticed.
They could tell I wasn't ok.
They could tell I needed help.

It was that moment I knew how lucky I was.
Even though I had never felt lower,
never felt more alone,
I had people who that mattered to.

Who asked questions,
who fought for me to fight my circumstance.

And how beautiful is that?

- *friendship*

I'm afraid to be real.
I'll pretend to like what others do.

All out of the fear that shadows me:
I don't want to be too much.

When asked, "who are you?"
I don't know the answer.
Or do I,
I'm just not comfortable with who that is?

I'm shy. I'm fickle. I'm emotional.
I can be lazy.
But then I won't sit still.
I love incredibly deeply. I let others influence me.
I'm seen as weak,
but I know I can be strong.
I'm a woman who wants a man she can stand by,
but who also stands by her.

I'm independent.
I'm stubborn.
I'm passionate.
I'm a storyteller.
I love my subtle dark side.

I might be a quiet spirit,

but that doesn't mean I'm weak.

That doesn't mean I don't know
how to stand up for myself.
It doesn't mean I don't care.
I'm selective of who comes into my life,
but those I do let in I will always fight for.
Always.

- when we learn from the bleeding

You stood idle as chaos ran around you.
You stood idle even when I begged you to follow.
You stood idle as I cried out in desperation.
You stood idle as you watched me drive away.

And you never came after me.
And I prayed that you would.
And I still do.

    - you wanted me to leave

It's like the wind got knocked out of me.
I forgot how to stand.
I forgot how to breathe.
My lungs didn't know what to do.
My head was fuzzy and my heart was tired.

So tired.

- conflict

It attacks for so long before you realize.
It's an enemy that seems harmless.
Before long, your decisions aren't your own.
They're made for someone else.
Your life is hinged to theirs.
You're lost apart from it.
It owns you.

- *codependency*

If I put up this boundary,
are you going to run away?
If I say no,
are you going to leave me?
If I stand up for myself,
does that mean losing you?

*- your boundaries don't scare away the people
you're meant to be around*

What if I can change?
I built my life around you,
before I realized I used the wrong kind of brick.
I let my walls come down,
for someone who wasn't willing to break them down.
For someone who didn't want the messy parts of me.
Who only wanted the cookie cutter,
who only wanted the me I showed the world.
I let my walls down and he walked away.

- ***some people you are meant to outgrow***

Summer.

You have your own closet.
You stare at me every day.
You bring memories of friendship,
of happiness,
of loneliness.
Of wondering.

That feeling of forever waiting.

- all of my bridesmaid dresses

So often we hide from the person we are.
Because it's easy,
to fit the cookie cutter mold,
surrounded by examples we can shape
to make our own.
And that makes it easy to blame.

- *society hoax*

Sometimes, it's the time to wait.
And sometimes, it's the time to make things happen.

- a choice

I was sheltered.
Made to believe I was unbreakable.
Then my limits were tested.
My comfort zones shattered.
My mind a mess, my heart in pieces.

I went into the world and it rejected me.
And I couldn't be more grateful.

- learning from each broken piece

I'm sick of losing sleep.
Sick of acting like the victim.
Sick of missing the narcissism.

Where would I be without you?
Closure.

- inner monologue

You walked my way.
Slowly.
Not intentionally.
Very unexpectedly.

You snuck up on me before I could run.
I didn't realize what was happening.

Do you know what you're doing to me?
Is it hard to sleep?
Because I feel an ache every day.
I actually feel a force, trying as it might,
to push me forward.
To keep me moving.

What I want to know,
is do you feel that too?

And do you know what you're doing to me?

- *diet*

My faith is the driving force of everything I do.
I need someone to walk that life with me.
Side by side.

   - let others know what's important to you

I'm a private person.
I don't desire to open my heart over and over again.
I occasionally live my life as a planner,
but I'm not always careful about who I commit to.
I'm attracted to mystery.
To a little darkness.

Because I know I'm not fully seen
when there isn't any light.

 - greatest fear

You were right in front of me,
but then you were gone.
And I'm not done yet.
You have to keep moving with me.
You've got to hold on.

To the memories,
to the laughter,
to the love I know you feel.
To everything you keep saying isn't real.

You tell me, "It's fake."
"It's just in your head."

I stood in your shadow,
crying as the wind pushed me around.
Pushing me back to where the trees laughed
and the sun kissed our skin while under its light.

And you told me I was right...

"It wasn't fake."
"It wasn't just in your head."

It's real and it's here.
It's you and it's me.
But now time has passed,

and you were gone.

- holding on when I should have let go

It's not a weakness.
It's the strength to expose the deepest,
darkest parts of yourself.
It's confidence.
It's the mirror in which we peer into everyday,
and becoming accepted.

- *vulnerability*

It runs so deep.
I think about it first thing every morning.

I don't share it.
I know once it's out,
that means I have to fix it.
And I don't want to.

It's my little secret.
The control I know I have.
And I don't want to let it go.

But I get mad when I step out of my own line.
I feel panicked
when I let in something I've sworn away.

I panic and I cry,
and I punish myself with abstinence.

I'm not ready to let it go.
And I still ask the same question each morning.

How do I need to eat today
to make sure I don't gain a thing?

 - what is this enemy?

Following your heart is a real strength.
Yes, you could get hurt,
but my darling, what if you only get stronger?

   - take that chance

I was cookie cutter.
I was a pleaser.
I am a pleaser.
I am a good girl.
And I hate that phrase.

- you aren't what people assume you to be

Take baby steps.
Jump into the deep end.
That secret you feel buries you.
You're not alone.

Tell the world.
Or just one person.
Whichever you choose,
you are right.

- you get to choose who you open up to

I look at others and I'm jealous.
Of how they don't overthink when going out.
Of how they don't care the calorie count.
As if they don't regret the choice
before they've even ordered.

Saying over and over,
trying so desperately to convince themselves.
"I really don't need food today."
And sometimes, most times,
that evil, evil thought.
It wins.

   - *this runs deep*

Vulnerability brings music.
Music is not always melodies and lyrics.
It can be conversation.
Conversations that flow lyrically.
A harmonizing experience.
A therapeutic fix to an otherwise impossible feeling.

- sit in friendship, trust in friendship

Top down,
sun setting,
wind strong.
The laughter infectious,
my heart completely full.
Surrounded by friendship,
and dogs in the car,
it was a good Tuesday evening.

- *the days memories are made*

I didn't know I'd miss it,
until it wasn't near.
It weaves,
and crashes,
and remains calm.
It can choose to be distant,
or decide to be close.
It's all of nature.
It's strong and it's still.
Like how I was taught to be.

- the ocean

Fight for your dreams, because no one else will.
Make life one hell of a story.

- make it one you're proud to tell

Fall.

I met you in October.
There were winding streets
and orange sunsets.

There were feelings
as we strolled through the bookstore
with charm in their pages
that matched my sweater all the more.

There was tequila.
There was magic.
It was Fall.
And I felt life was changing alongside the leaves.

    - october

Today, I choose thankfulness.
Thankful for the chaos and confusion.
Thankful for newness.
Thankful for endurance.
Thankful for Sundays with sunshine.
And a surrendered chaos.

Honey, your soul is golden.

- your soul is the light we see

I have never believed in love at first sight.
But I knew the moment I saw you,
we would have a story.
When I glanced in your direction,
I could see a future clearly.
I have never believed in love at first sight.
But I knew from the very first moment,
I'd belong with you, for at least a little while.

   - a moment I knew

Challenge me.
Think differently.
Desire to learn.

I hope you like my creative thinking.
I want you to see it as sexy.
Because that is me for me.

It makes all the difference,
when I'm fully who I love to be.

- me for me

I want to dance with you.
The totally cheesy kind.
The kind where you twirl me through empty streets
at night to no music.
The kind when you hold me close
and make it feel like the world is standing still.
The kind where all I hear are heartbeats.

I want those romantic nights.
The just sort of happen nights.
I want the kind of nights that let me know,
you and I are real and forever.

    - a daydream

You were my autumn of daydreams.
Just five more minutes.
Five more minutes so I can dream of you.
I just need five more minutes.
To forever freeze this memory, to cover it in blue.
Blue skies overhead,
blue waves crashing into it all,
the blue of my Vans and the winter to come.

I think of blue gatorade,
how it's the only kind you'll drink.
Just five more minutes,
and let me daydream of you.

I just need five more minutes,
so I can forget it all too.

    - the color blue

I can't walk this life alone.
Many times, I feel I do,
but I have this fire inside me.
This spirit of love and strength and purpose.

I have a Father who loves me,
cherishes me,
moves me and keeps me still.

I get to rest knowing it's not all on me.
It's with the One who cares more for my life
than any man could.

- *faith*

I was with you because I was lonely.
I looked to you for validation.
For real love.
But that wasn't fair to you.
You never promised me forever.
You never promised me a present.
I put this label on you,
on what I assumed we would be.
Even though you never said,
"Yes, I want a you and a me."

I'm learning it slowly.
What this season is teaching.
I deserve more,
and you want something different.

    *- **i hold blame too***

I'm just going to bury it deep.
I'm going to pretend it's not on my mind,
in pieces and shattered.

I'm wandering nowhere.
I'm stuck in a rut that I won't climb out of.
I'm holding back what I want out of fear.

You'll get punched,
you'll get bruised,
you'll feel pain as chaos ensues.

And it's because you're alive.
You hurt because your heart beats.
You'll fight because you're worth it.

You can overcome, because it's what you do.

- believing your own strength

My feet may get me there,
but it's your words that carry me.
Your independence,
your loyalty and grace.
The sacrifices you make for me,
despite my fickle history.
The worry you link to me,
I wish you'd let go.
I'm ok,
because you loved me.

- *mothers*

You miss all your friends
as they move away.
As people get married,
and promoted,
and scattered.
It gets harder,
when you get older.

- age

I just want to yell,
"Figure things out so I can love you."
Learn to speak up,
when it's something I need to hear.
Will you believe me,
when I say you matter to me?

- please, please, let me love you

You buy me hard cider.
You listen when I speak.
You watch me when you think I can't see.

You know God leads my steps,
that my mind never slows down,
that french fries warm my heart.

You describe me as subtle, yet loud.

You are kindness and you are joy.
You are hardworking and you are selfless.

You are my person,
who gets taken by the waves.

- sailor

I want the new.
The pure and the magic.
A child-like wonder,
that endless desire.

I want to walk that road with you.
Dance in the rain with you.
Stand in love and all that's true.
Stand as one, as we were always meant to.

- sometimes I get lost in the past

Find the one who makes you feel like an adventurer.
Who makes you feel like a conqueror.
The one who makes you feel safe, but also a little dirty.

The one you want to be with at two in the morning.
And two in the afternoon.
The one who gives you his sweater just because,
and dances with you even though he's shy.

He is soft and gentle and kind.
He likes you when you're quiet,
and even more so when you're loud.
He is easy to love,
he laughs often,
he grins like a child,
but kisses like a man.

He isn't your everything, but he is your forever.

- the imperfect two of us

Some need constant companionship,
others prefer solitude.
Respect that.

- listen

Comfort.
Peace.
Emotion.
Anxiety.
Trauma.
Memories.
How can you be all those things at once?

- childhood home

My heart burns for it.
My head gets lost in it.
My feet will one day walk it.
I dream of city lights.

- the big city

You're the one
I want to get drunk on Wednesday night with,
and go for a run on Saturday morning with.
You're the time I want to spend.
The effort I want to give.
The love I want to feel.

   - all of what I can give I want to give to you

The person who knows you fully.
The one who knew your secrets
before they were secrets.
The best friend you never intended,
but am so happy nature decided to gift.
An advocate.
An annoyance.
A safe place.
A soulmate.

    - a sibling

Your 6am wake ups.
The smell of blueberry muffins.
Mom's voice in the morning.
Dad's records blaring.
Your little brother's laugh.

Remember the small.
They are what make the big.

- the little things

She began walking.
Not stopping to question it, not daring to talk.

She felt calm.
She started to realize,
she'd get through it all.

The burden, the pain,
the terrible fear that she'd crumble and disappear.

Her future was clawing and fighting,
pushing her towards what she was scared of,
but completely deserved.

She looked out at a world she didn't recognize,
but who welcomed her like an old friend.
She had been fighting progress,
had been fighting independence,
afraid of being alone.
But there she stood,
atop what she had been climbing far too long.

She was scared and unsure.
But she walked anyways.
Knowing the unknown was far better
than what she had before.

- a breakthrough

Winter.

Yes, this is a love story.
But it's touch and go.
It's not linear,
but it's effortless.
It's not perfect,
but it's mine.

One that will follow me,
relentlessly and beautifully,
wherever I may go.

- *a welcomed shadow*

What a plot twist you were.

- the unexpected and wonderful

Who gets your trust,
your energy and soul?
It's enviable, daunting, terrifying,
and wonderful.
It's important and yours to give.
Hold it for someone who sees you completely,
and leans in all the more.

- *discernment*

Pull me out of my shell.
Make me curious.
Be confident.
Explore and try new things.
You never know what you can find
when you're no longer comfortable.

- *desires*

Everyone is nice.
Very few are kind.
Someone who is unafraid to share their world.
Someone who is intentional with your heart.
Someone who is honest with how you make them feel.
Those are to be cherished.

- **kindness**

Don't say it's too late.
Don't say it's too expensive.
Don't say you're not ready.

You never will be.
That's why they call it taking a leap of faith,
not a leap of certainty.

- just do something

I'm worth more than a quarter of your attention.
I'm more than an afterthought.

If you choose me,
then choose me.
To know me, all of me.

- i'd rather have rejection than ingenuity

It's ok to say no.
It's ok to put yourself first.
It's ok to be bold.
It's ok to be wrong.
It's ok to fight for something
everyone else tosses away.

It's ok to sit in silence.
It's ok to be loud.
It's ok to be different.

It's ok, just being you.

- *no apologies*

My grace is sufficient for you.
My grace is sufficient for you.
My grace is sufficient for you.

- *Jesus*

I will fight for you.
For the future I can see clearly.
These are feelings I don't want to disappear.
I want to be where we've already said those words,
where life moves forward,
with us intertwined.

- obstacles you're willing to fight

Step away from the office.
Spend time with the people you love.
Sing carols loudly and poorly.
Cheer with eggnog,
and then pour it down the sink,
because that stuff is just gross.
Don't take time for granted.
It passes by so much quicker than you think.

- *holidays*

Gingerbread lattes.
Cute boots.
Big scarves.
Fireplaces.
Snowball fights.
Plaid flannel.
Old knitted blankets (lots of them).
James Taylor.

I love Christmas.

- what happy looks like to me

You're going to make it.

- and you're going to be ok

We walked out of the bar at 2am.
The air was cold, but I felt warm.
Something in my heart was bright.

Our hands were intertwined,
our smiles lovingly painted
as we walked on cobblestone.

You twirled me in the street as the city made no sound.
You told me over and over, made the declaration loud.

But silence followed that night.
After your fear set in, after letting your truth come out.
Your insecurities broken, everywhere.
My memory of that moment,
you disappeared and shut it down.
I couldn't break the ache that I felt,
that never-ending sting.

It felt like burning.
It felt like change would never come.

And then all at once, november became spring.

- ***november became spring***

Spring.

There are seasons of everything.
Of pain and of joy.
Friendship and loss.
Promotions and setbacks.
Travels and stillness.

Each year begins with flowers.
And then sunshine.
And then change.
And then death.

But then the flowers grow again.

- let every season in

I'm still being mended.
I'm learning,
I'm growing,
I'm becoming myself.
Finally.
Heart, taking courage.
Head, keeping straight.
Life, bringing me sunshine and rain.

   - perseverance

The ones who inspire,
they're the ones who endure.

They've been beaten,
bruised,
tested,
and judged through it all.
The ones that have the life they truly want,
because they fought for it.

Focused.
Driven.
Passionate.

No matter if you're 18 or 85.
Find something you care about and care deeply.

- and don't let anyone take that away from you

Figures.
Ghosts.
Souls.

In life, you find people.
You find people who love you.
Who teach you,
who challenge you,
and who hurt you.

Those people make you grow in a way no one else can.
They teach you discernment.
They teach you to guard your heart.
Let that be a priceless lesson.

- every person has a purpose

You break and you heal.
You fall and you rise.

Just look at the waves.
Look at the stars.
Sometimes we feel we can't go backwards
once we've moved forward.
But healing is personal.
Healing is anything but linear.

- let yourself heal with grace

I love what you make me.
I love what I make you.
I love us.

    - I love us

I already miss you.
Even before you're gone,
I feel what it's like when you're absent.
Like that Sunday night feeling,
knowing Monday creeps up slowly.
My heart's happy, but breaking.
Knowing that when the sun rises,
I'll wake up alone.

   - long distance

You are stronger than the grief that buries you.
You are kinder than the cruel situations.
You are powerful amidst agony.
You can cry out and be heard.
Give yourself permission to fall apart.
You have the tools to piece back together.

   - rebuilding

I have to thank you.
I'd rather have loved you once than never at all.

Falling in love with you,
it's just pieces of a song.
That I try to write,
that I always feel.
They creep and they sneak
and they break and they mend.
Over and over again.

Now I know what my heart is capable of.
And how truly strong I am.

   - piecing back together

Let's talk about the good things.
Feel free in stillness.
And in the storms.

I want to encourage you,
to talk about what you push down.

To remember that just on the other side of darkness,
is so much light.

- *in your own time*

There is only one you.
Only one personality exactly like yours.

Make it one people remember as kindness.

   - ***only one you***

Invincible at 18.
Lost at 22.
Broken at 25.
Healing at 27.
...

    - consistently growing

A LETTER TO A GOOD MAN.

It's you and me. setting sail into the world. While many people think we're crazy to believe in this adventure, I find it comforting. I've always been a step ahead of others, out of sync, beating my own drum and following my own thoughts. And you've always been direct. Following your head, the strong things, the, "stuff of men" as you try to convince me it's called. And while that last bit I'd like to fight at times, I respect how focused you can be. how driven and purposeful and intentional you are with the words you speak and the steps you take.

It's how I know and trust the way you feel for me.

You and I are so, so similar. and yet, you're foreign to me. you're a trusted mystery. A fickle & stable person. You are kindness and joy. sternness and patience.

Adventurous and scheduled. Simple and oh so complex.

We talk about the future until 4am. You buy me prosecco. You always share your fries. You never let me forget what it's like to feel your touch. You make me feel safe. And a little bit dirty. I never told you how much I cherish that.

We each fall in love with every dog on the street. we order tacos and drink until the morning begins to wake. I get up early and watch as your chest slowly rises and falls. I make us both coffee while the sun still sleeps with you. your sweater around my arms, the scent of you as close as it can be. the songs of Wild Rivers play in my head as I slip by and watch the stillness of the city through the hotel window.

these are the happy memories of us. this is magic to me. and when you finally wake, you search for me, and then you smile. good gracious. you make my heart go wild.

About the Author

Kyle Erin was born in Norfolk, Virginia and moved all over as a military child, eventually settling in Jacksonville, Florida. She completed her Master's degree in Publishing from George Washington University in May 2021 and currently works as a freelance editor and assistant in both academic and trade atmospheres. She still resides in Northern Virginia, and this will be her debut publication.